REPORTED FOR DUTY

Poems and Stories from the War Zone, Home Front, and Beyond

Featuring Poetry and Prose by

Michael Lewis Beesley • Dawn Clayton
John Clayton • Jon Freeland • John T. Grady II
Donald (Bob) Jahr • Mathew Lee • Jason Mayer
Corey Phillips • William (Bill) Tracy

Edward Gehlert, Jason Mayer, and John Clayton
Editors

Happy Duck Publishing
111 East 3rd Street
Belle, MO 65013

Genre: Poetry, General
ISBN: 978-0-9861182-9-6
First Edition.

For Those Who Served and Those Who Love Them

WOUNDED WARRIOR PROJECT®

Table of Contents

John Clayton was drafted into the U.S. Army in 1968 and volunteered for an additional year to gain training in electronics.

He served in Vietnam from April 1969 to October 1970. He repaired weather equipment at Firebase Black Hawk in II Core and at LZ Sandy.

After military service, John earned a BS in Education from the University of Missouri at Columbia. He then taught school at Belle, Missouri for three years before entering the University of Missouri School of Law at Columbia and earning a Juris Doctorate. He became a partner in the law firm of Thomas, Birdsong, Clayton and Haslag, PC and practiced law in Rolla, Missouri for seventeen years. In 1997 he was appointed to fill the Associate Circuit Court judge vacancy in Maries County, Missouri and he served in that position for thirteen years.

John has been married to Dawn for forty-six years. They have four children and fifteen grandchildren. They live in rural Maries County, Missouri.

Why Me

I have strong feelings in my heart.
They have been mixed from the start.
Proud of bravery in I Drang, many died.
Ashamed of the cowardly carnage in Mei Lei.

Random death, no reason why.
Luck determines if you die.
Virgil walked point 127 days.
He was strange, he had his ways.

Virgil's body came home whole.
But his heart was cold.
His wife and kids never knew what would raise his ire.
For Virgil was always looking for the trip wire.

Mickey was the Colonel's aide.
He made sure everyone was paid.
That job seemed safe enough.
Till an RPG gave him the snuff.

You just never know which way luck's gonna go.
Good luck is good, ain't it Joe?
But in the back of our mind, we wonder why,
We got through and did not die.

We feel a little guilty when we think about the wall.
How did we get so lucky as not to fall?
Just put your head down and plow on your way.
All you have to do is make it through, another day.

Sometimes, we just wonder why.
Perhaps we deserve to fry.
Death will come when it's time to die.
There's really no reason to wonder why.

Good Luck Bad Luck

Chopper noises are all around
Stretchers sitting on the ground
Blood seeping into the dirt
But Jim Bo Krenshaw does not hurt

It has been a real hard day
Pain and death is what we pay
Going back to base camp now
With only sadness on our brow

Sitting on empty ammo cases
Not thinking about safer places
Don't bogart that joint my friend
Pass it over here again

Hot, wet, dirty and tired
We lost a little soul each time we fired
Hollowed eyes, exhausted faces
Dink ears on boot laces

Not for ideals, not for home
Hoping to avoid a cold tombstone
Not for God or apple pie
Just trying not to die

102 days of luck to go
247 days of luck to go
173 days of luck to go
He ran out of luck, Ole Jim Bo.

It Never Goes Away

OCTOBER 1970
When I stepped out of that plane in Seattle
   I thought I had left the Nam behind.
All safe and sound, nothing more to battle.
Just chase the girls, and they were looking fine.
Go right home? I don't think so.
I can go to Montana and spend a little dough.

I have heard some guys were treated badly.
That was not my experience.
It was not people that left me tense.
It was memories that no one understood.
It was nerves right on top of the skin,
   that put me into hiding at the drop of a pin.
A sound, the whisper of leaves, wind in the grass,
   just about anything could make me show my ass.
"Why do you try to take my head off when I touch you,
   it's only time to go?"
"To wake me up, just wiggle my toe."
"Why don't you ever talk,
   and never like company when you take a walk?"
John to self, you've got to get it under control.
Don't think about it. Don't think about it.
It's ruining my life, all this shit.
Just block it out. Just block it out.
Just put it in a box, put it in a box,
   close the lid and snap shut the lock.
Now that's a relief!
Some how it feels good to slink away like a thief.

OCTOBER 1985

15 years out, I am better without a doubt.
No more diving under tables when a car backfires.
I hid it pretty well, I think I'm able
    to be pretty normal, putting out fires
      that come up in life.

OCTOBER 1990

20 years out,
    in a quiet time, those memories, I can think about.
I can put in the key and turn the lock,
    raise the lid and take a memory out.
I can turn them this way and that
    and upside down.
Nobody ever knows because I don't make a sound.
For the next 28 years, I think I am on a streak.
Any time I like, I can open the box and take a peek.

FEBRUARY 2018

The theater is dark like a shroud,
   the sound is turned up very loud.
Daniel Ellsberg is dressed in green,
   with an infantry platoon, on the screen.
You can hear the boots moving through the grass.
Water drips from bamboo onto wide, green leaves,
   shinning like glass.
Everyone in the movie is quiet, the theater is tense.
No talking in the movie or in the theater.
Suspense!
It's very quiet. Only the plop of water droplets
   on leaves.

CLACKETY, CLACKETY, CLACKETY,
   the metallic clack of an AK 47 opens up.
Suddenly there is a chaos of sound.
M16s, AKs, an M60 and maybe a Thumper,
   gunfire and yelling all around.
I am there.
In the Nam.
Heart pounding.
Hands trembling.
Body shaking.
Short of breath.
A death grip on my non-existent M-16.
In the middle of the afternoon!
In the afternoon!
In Florida, for crying out loud!
God damnit! God damnit!
Where did this come from?

Marvin Parker, You Son-of-a-Bitch

You are a ghost
 but don't think I've forgotten you, Marvin Parker.
"You son-of-a-bitch!"

I never thought about you much
 before that army car
 pulled into the driveway.
Oh, I heard you had been drafted,
 but didn't think about it much .

When those two soldiers in dress uniforms
 asked where your folks lived.
In that instant I knew you were dead.
I had not done anything wrong
 but you made me feel guilty.

"You son-of-a-bitch!"

Me with my college deferment.
Me only having to worry about buying gas
 and paying for fees and books.
Me not worrying about people being killed 8,000 miles away.
Me not thinking about duty.
Not thinking about honor.
Not thinking about freedom.
Not thinking about fairness.
Marvin Parker, you changed all of that.

"You son-of-a-bitch!"

It was you that made my stomach knot up when others
    demonstrated.
It was you that made me feel guilty for being alive.
It was you that made me abandon that college deferment.
It was you Marvin Parker, or maybe your ghost.

"You son-of-a-bitch!"

I heard that to vanquish your demons,
    you must confront them.
Where better to do that than the wall.

There it is.
Dark.
Shiny.
Brooding.
Names etched on every part.
Bodies, each and every one.
Stacked in long, neat rows.

"You son-of-a-bitch!"

Tears streaming down my face.
You make me cry in public,
    and in front of my wife.
I don't like that!
Get out of my life.

"You son-of-a-bitch!"

The setting sun reflects on the wall,
    spreading across the names.
Orange and black blood oozes down the granite.
My fingers trace your name.

I see my face in the wall,
    but my name is not there.
I see your face in the wall.
Not a soldier's face.
It's the face of a high school kid,
    with pimples and a scraggly mustache.
Shaggy brown hair flopped over your right eye.

My hand feels wet.
I pull it back, expecting to see blood.
It is not. It has started raining.
I turn to leave. Take a step and turn back.
I say to the wall, "You stay here Marvin Parker."

"You son-of-a-bitch!"

It Takes Money to Buy Whiskey

This Vietnam veteran knows that heroes are few and far
    between,
But we have them, they can be seen.
Doyle, Inouye, Kerry and McCain
On their honor, not one stain.
Vets are just people, like everyone they say.
Well, at least, we started out that way.
Combat changes you, that I know.
Sometimes my mind wanders, not knowing where to go.
Veterans, please stand to be honored, to be honored by all.
I will not stand, that takes some gall.
No! I will not stand for you, who will not pay taxes for a vets
    medical care.
Say it to my face, you would not dare.
Oh, you are here now, that you are too old to go.
When it was your time, your legs had a bow.
Our BRAVE president, who causes GOP hearts to stir,
When it was his turn, bought a bone spur.
Where were you, when my world was quaking?
Where were you when I woke up at night, sweating and
    shaking?
Where were you when I could not concentrate enough to work?
You said I was just a drunk and a jerk.
That mental health treatment just cost too much,
    that taxes will not reach,
And with that you turned me on to the street.
There is nothing wrong with him, that he didn't choose.
He's just lazy and likes his booze.
He's no good, on that you can bet.
Just walk on by that dirty old vet.
Trumpites are feeling frisky,
But it takes money to buy whiskey.

You say vets are heroes, that's what you say,
But not what you do,
When it comes time to pay.
Stand up veterans, look at me shine!
When more taxes are needed, we'll see if you have a spine.

My Sister

* Note to reader: The words "bo di" are many Vietnam veterans' version of "scram" in Vietnamese.

He stood on a pile of rock
As we rolled into Pleiku.
He danced around like a fighting cock.

**"Hey, GI. My sista fuck you.
My sista, 5 dolla, GI."**
"You little bastard, bo di."

He was 10 and looked 6.
Dirty, hungry, and skinny as a stick.
He was bare foot, a booney hat on his head.

"Hey, GI. My sista gotta bed."
*"You little Gook, are your ears full of shit.
Didn't you hear me when I said git!"*

He was desperate and could not go,
Even if it meant pissing off Joe.

*"Get this convoy to moving, man.
This kid is more than I can stand."*

"Come on GI, my sista, 3 dolla, GI."
He said with a tear in his eye.

*"Bo di, bo di, bo di.
God dammit kid, do you want to die?
We're going to hell. We're going to fry."*

"My sista, 2 dolla, GI."

I thought to myself as we went on our way.
"Shit, I'll never forget this hateful day."

The Box

I had to put you in a box.
To which only I can have a key.
I had to put you in a box,
So I am the only one who can see.

It was necessary you know.
I had to come back to the world,
And into society go.
No one could see the pain and anguish that in my heart swirled.

When your fate was found.
Near Mang Yang Pass in II Core,
By a single mortar round.
They took your life Jack, and never knew they even made a score.

That box is in my heart, where only I can see.
When I am alone, I put it in the lock
And then I turn the key,
And out you come with the other memories.

We can visit and talk and shoot the breeze and then it is time to go.
We have to keep it secret Jack, no one else must know.
That little trick keeps me safe from what we did so many years ago.
That stuff would make my family afraid, you know.

Jack it's time to get back in the box.
What do you mean you're not ready to go?
Damn it, Jack, get back in the box.
You know I have to go.

Default on the Debt

AGENT ORANGE

It's not an agent and it's not orange.
It is dioxin. That's a real toxin.
They sprayed it from the air.
They sprayed it in our hair.

It made the trees drop their leaves.
Those trees were bare if you please.
It made the rice wilt into the water.
Not good for food. Not fit for fodder.

What about the people.
If you don't die today.
What about the people.
Well it's worth it they say.

They are dying like flies.
VA hospitals are full of these guys.
Come on America, help them out.

Deny! Deny! Deny!
More of them must die.
Too many Vets would benefit,
If we were to admit it.
We cannot do it.
We just cannot afford it.

GULF WAR SYNDROME

They really are sick.
They actually die.
Get on the stick.
It doesn't matter if you know why.

It could be depleted uranium.
Or maybe the Sand Fever Fly.
Could be biological agents,
Raining down from the sky.

Maybe 600 oil wells on fire,
That put Vets on the funeral pyre.
It doesn't matter if we know why,
What matters is that they die.

What matters is that they and their families pay,
Just trying to get through another day.

Deny! Deny! Deny!
More of them must die.
Too many Vets would benefit,
If we were to admit it.
We cannot do it.
We just cannot afford it.

CHRONIC TRAUMATIC ENCEPHALOPATHY

Just think of it as brain butter.
No! No! I did not stutter.
As gross as that may seem.

Un-homogenized cream
Being slapped around in a jar
Makes that tasty dream.
Fat molecules stick together.
Ah! Butter.

Explosions shake the skull jar.
The brain, sweet cream of humankind,
Gets slapped around in the skull jar.
Tau proteins stick to others that they find.
Yuck! Brain butter.

Brain butter kills the brain,
A little at a time, like potholes kill a car.
Just a little bit, each and every hour.
In the end the Vet and family suffer,
But all we hear is the refrain.

Deny! Deny! Deny!
More of them must die.
Too many Vets would benefit,
If we were to admit it.
We cannot do it.
We just cannot afford it.

War Talk

What did you do in the war?
No answer.
I'd really like to know, Sir.
No answer.
Can't you just tell them?
No answer.
Not a thing from the heart of him.
No answer.
He doesn't want them to know.
There's blood on his hands.
He wouldn't want them to go;
To fight in other lands.
He doesn't talk about what he did, when he was only a kid.
They wouldn't see him the same way.
He thinks it best to keep on the lid,
And leave all this talk for another day.

The Vet

He sat between the trailers that offered a screen.
He needed to be outside, but didn't want to be seen.
*"I don't know why man.
It's just something I can't stand.*

*It don't make no sense
But people make me tense.
Ever since Iraq
I can't take people lookin' at my back."*

Do Not

Do not.
Just,
Just do not.
Just do not tell me,
Just do not tell me you are too tired.
Too tired to care,
Too tired to pay attention.
Too tired to pay attention,
    To what happened today.
Too tired to listen to disheartening news.
Too tired to hear another lie.

Just
Just   too   tired
Just   too   tired   to   listen
Just too tired to hear another speech
    without a complete sentence.
Another day of puking out Sean Hannity.
Another day of blaming sick people,
    For being sick.
Another day of blaming poor people,
    For being poor.

Another day of corporate subsidies.
Another day of farm subsidies.
Another day of offshore accounts.
Another day of taking food from kids,
    So the rich can get richer.

Do not!
Just do not!
Just do not thank me for my service.
Just do not thank me for my service,
　　If you cannot muster the energy,
　　to listen.

The energy to pay attention.
The energy to be pissed.
The energy to look your neighbor in the eye.
To look your neighbor in the yes and say,
　　"This is wrong."
　　"This is immoral."
　　"This hurts America."

Just do not thank me for my service,
　　If you are too damn lazy to vote.
Just　Do　Not!

The Yellow Stripe

I saw you look down.
Like you are searching for something on the ground.
I guess you're just not that strong.
I know, you know, what he said is wrong.

You talk about honor
   and doing the right thing.
Then when you're out of sight, around the corner
   and all that big talk doesn't mean a thing.

What's holding you back?
What do you lack?
I think I see it,
   that wide yellow stripe running down your back.
I'm pretty sure that's what you lack.

You're a weak kneed sissy.
A whole lot of wispy,
A coward at best.
A big old pussy like all the rest.

You talk a lot of smack
   but can't keep it on track.
Just pull off your shirt, so we all can see,
   that big yellow stripe running down your back.

He Deserves a Purple Heart

A Purple Heart
Should be on his shirt
From the start
When he hit the dirt
He answered the call
He honored the draft
He didn't try to stall
Fighting was not his craft
He did what was required
With the rifle he fired
He knew from the start
GI's get shot through the heart
No broken bones
Tears like a flood
There is not loss of blood
It's the soul that is dead

The Crying Wall

(For John Dorsey)

The wall is a place where people cry.
Not just kids who are handicapped and tired.
The spirits of young men linger and I know why.
They were not ready to go, they did not want to die.

You do not need to know a name on that wall,
For the souls of dead boys to make the tears fall.
Some places make me feel bad,
But the wall makes me feel sad.

I saw it first in 87 on a trip for work,
17 years after I got back to the World.
I had no space for emotion, I just wanted to work.
There were protesters, but with them I had no quarrel.

As I walked down, into that hole,
It was reflex that my fingers traced his name.
I felt a bit of air. It was cold.
I know it was the breath of a human soul.

I felt overwhelmingly sad.
Tears streamed down my face.
I felt so, so sad.
There is just something about that place.

Those tears had been in the box.
That granite monolith pried open the lid.
On the ground at the apex was a pair of plaid socks.
I was a hardened man, not a kid.

It took some time to get those emotions back in the box.
In my line of work, emotional is not a good style.
It puts a smile on my face when I think about those socks.
I have not been back to the wall, but I think about it once in a while.

Why Vets Don't Talk

Why don't Vets ever talk?
Oh, they have plenty to say.
Vets do talk.
It's just not what's interesting to you.
They talk about their kids, wives, and football too.

Most people don't want to hear,
About that cold hand on their heart that puts them in fear.
Most people want to see the gore and stretch their neck,
Like adolescent boys who come on to a wreck.

Most Vets know you really don't care.
You just want to gawk and have a good stare.
Vets are not people who whine.
If you want to help a Vet,
Just sit with them, and spend some time.

Kim Lee

* The Douglas A-1 Skyraider was nick named Spad after the famous WWI French fighter plane.

You've been had by a Spad dad!
That was the brag back at the base.
At 22, a fighter plane jock, he thought he was bad!
They're the same the world over, every place.

When you kill from afar,
At first it's like they're on a star.
A far, far away star.
But on the subconscious, it leaves a scar.

You've been had by a Spad dad!
You take them out on your way in,
Or the missiles do you in, on your way out.
There she was chained to a poinsettias sprout.

The look on her face put a chill down his spine.
There she was directly in line.
What in the hell, do you do?
Either you take out the missile, or the missile takes out you.

The look on her face said she knew she would die.
Training told him, drop the bomb, you have to try.
He made it back to base, not so cocky this time.
The chill down his back didn't go away with time.

She was always with him, she wouldn't let him be.
He saw her so much, he named her Kim Lee.
He left the military, he ran away far.
But there she was on the windshield of his car.

He tried and tried and went to the VA.
No amount of drugs made Kim Lee go away.
50 years later when he prays, for his soul to keep,
There's Kim Lee as he tries to sleep.

What's it Like?

Some experiences are personal.
They are not describable by the spoken word.
If you really want to know, you will just have to do it.
There ain't no short cut, to it.

What's it like to have a baby?
What's it like to feel pain in a missing foot?
What's it like to ask for their hand in marriage and get a maybe?
What's it like to lose all your loot?

What's it like to have your mother die?
What's it like to realize your sweetheart has told you a lie?
What's it like to believe you are about to die?
What's it like to kill someone and watch them die?

What's it like to have PTSD?
Well you never know what the next time will be.
We'll just have to wait and wait and wait and see.
No one else's words can set you free.

What is combat like, they want to know.
Well, put your fear in a box, and let it go.
I'm too busy right now to let it show.
And if I don't die, maybe, just maybe, I will grow.

The Bible says you should expect to reap what you sow.
We poets do our best to take you where we go.
We can write the descriptive words and try and try.
But we still do not know what it's like to die.

His Body Made it Home

Today, as I put up flags for the Lions Club,
To honor those who never made it home.
I thought of my father, who did make it home.
My father whose body came home.

My father whose soul and mind never made it off that island.
My father who, at times, would cry and rage,
Against "those yellow bastards,
Who ate our boys like they were livestock."

My father who could not put it in a box for long.
Who could not keep the lid closed.
The lid on that box would fly open,
And the demons would come clamoring out.

To smother his reality,
To block out the sun of success,
And family.
People say that some Vets are just weaker than others.

That may be true,
But when America calls its citizens to war,
It does not inquire if their souls are shielded,
By armor plate or egg shells.

My Father's War

We all just thought he was crazy and mean.
What was paranoia or so it seemed,
I now know was hyper-vigilance.

Ambulance driving and blood in streams
were always present in his dreams.
Then there were the burial details,
Hauling bodies in dump trucks full to the rails.

Collecting dog tags from fallen GIs.
Using a bayonet amid the flies
digging for sweetheart lockets
in the pockets of humans, 7 days dead.

They laid them in rows, side by side
and bulldozers covered them with dirt from either side.
Okinawa, that was his war.
The rest of the Pacific seemed so far.

Shell shock was what they called it then.
PTSD was unknown to him.
Once in a while he had that thousand yard stare.
But only once in a while, it was pretty rare.

What we saw, was our father withdraw.
When times were really hard, it was the final straw.
It was weeks in bed, unable to move,
when there was little to eat and no wood for the stove.

I have often wondered, and still do not know,
why some Vets have to move on even in the snow.
For my father it was different, at least he thought so.
He didn't choose to leave town, God told him to go.

He never dealt with his PTSD.
He never understood, he just couldn't see.
At the end of his life, he talked about his experiences with me.
I hoped his talking would set him free.

I am not sure that talking so little could heal that scar.
PTSD sets a pretty high bar.
Vets struggle with it near and far.
My father died still fighting that war.

MILITARY CURRENCY

SERIES 100

錢拾

10 SEN

B

拾

A 16268893 A

B

TEN SEN

SERIES 100

10 SEN

Dawn Clayton is a housewife, mother of four children, grandmother of fifteen grandchildren, lawyer, and wife of a Vietnam Veteran for forty-five years. She is a long time resident of Maries County, Missouri.

Where Does He Go?

Where does he go behind those eyes
A place I cannot go
A place he will not let me go
He leaves for hours in the woods
A place he will not let me go
When this domestic scene is too much for him
He does not trust me or anyone
His walls are high and thick
Forty years by his side and I get a glimpse,
But only when he opens up,
To others of shared experience
I will continue to love him
One day he may let me go where he goes

Corey Phillips joined the U.S. Army in 1990 and served for three years as an All-Source Intelligence Analyst specializing in situational analysis.

He served in Korea with the 501st Military Intellegence Battalion then returned to Fort Huachuca, Arizona to be an instructor.

After leaving the Army in 1993, he spent twenty-five years working in the private security field. Today, he is a published author, voice actor, storm chaser, and leadership consultant with www.getgreattogether.com.

Corey currently is bringing a new digital shopping platform online for both Android and iPhone. He lives in Sullivan, Missouri with his wife Kathryn and his four children Emily, Ashley, Briana, and Christopher.

A Change of Scenery

Before the green
After the green
So many things change
Perspective, language, attitude
Nothing is the same
Tolerance and intolerance
Love and hate
Friends and foes
What is trust
What is love
I do know fear
I do know paranoia
Before the green
After the green
So many things have changed

Why I Hate Being a Vet... Sometimes

I once was proud to stand
When the call went out
I would always stand

I once was honored to applaud
Applaud with my fellow vets
As recognition was given

But not anymore

Being a Vet lately has become the cheapest of "Pops"
At a bad pro wrestling event
At baseball games
At monster truck rallies

When these events start to lose their crowd
Like a civilian who doesn't understand concealment
You can see it coming a mile away

"We would like to honor all our Vets and First Responders!
Please stand and let us honor you..."

You are not honoring us
You are exploiting us to get a reaction
A reaction from a dead audience

You commercialize us
Commercialize us to sell more food
To sell more soda and beer
To feel more American

You want to honor us?
Then don't forget why we served in the first place
To help the world gain freedom
Freedom from terror
From tyranny
From oppression

To preserve our Constitution
The Constitution that defines us

This is why we served
And why some died

Honor the cause
And you truly honor us

A Lonely Walk Back From Hooker Hill

Two months in country and so far from home.
No family,
No close friends,
My girl thousands of miles away.

Lonely is not a word,
But a way of life during a one-year tour.

We drink.
We go to the ville.
We drink some more.

In a staggered stumble back down Itaewon's steep decline.
It's namesake amongst us all calls out to me.
"Ya-ya, hey you come here!"

I feel the female arm slide around mine.
The smell of cheap knockoff perfume hits my nose.
"You lonely tonight?"
The voice asks...
Knowing all too well that we all are.

"$20 short time. Me make you feel like you back home."

In a drunken lonely haze...
That is all I long for.
I agree.

I follow her down a narrow alley,
Knowing all too well,
A mistake is about to be made.

"Shoes off here."
As we walk into a sorority house,
Home to the oldest profession on the planet.

A small low-lit room,
money is exchanged for my self-esteem,
My dignity,
My honor.

It's over.
No kiss, no hug.
Just a dingy washcloth to clean myself,
A finger pointing at the door.

I realize I must walk back down the same alley,
And back onto the street,
People passing by,
They all know where I have been,
Know what I have done,
Looking at me with judgmental eyes.

The walk back to my barracks is so long,
Each step a trudging ruck march of shame.

I know there is someone back home…
But they are so far away.

I know my mom would be upset…
But she is so far away.

My mind and my gut feel sick.
Not for what I have done,
But knowing that I am going back again tomorrow.

Tomorrow night I will take another long walk again.
A walk away from that low-lit room.
Away from my self-esteem,
My dignity,
My honor.

The Long Journey to the Bottom of a Bottle

New, nervous and way out of my element,
A young man reporting to his first duty station.

First is orientation,
Then duty that day,
Finally, a gathering beside the barracks,
BBQ in the air.

"Hey, new guy!"
Is shouted by the Senior NCO,
He is working the grill.
I am handed my first beer ever.

Three beers in,
A jug is brought out in my honor,
It reads Napoleon...

My ears are filled with jokes and laughter,
And stories from Soldiers who were there before.
My eyes too blurry to focus.
Am I yelling?
No.
Something is coming from my mouth though...
I hear laughter...
Then the darkness comes...

Something painful is perceived.
My body.
My Head.
My Stomach.
My Eyes...

The sun is bright as I am woken,
Woken by the same man who offered me the bottle.
"Hey, Soldier!
PT is in one hour you better get cleaned up!"

I had slept under unseen stars that night.
The platoon laughs hard.

During each exorcise I lurch,
Dry-heaving my way into acceptance.

A year has gone by,
Many bottles have been emptied.
Emptied from exploits.
Emptied from boredom.
Emptied from loneliness and the longing to go home.

I have three days left in-country,
My relief has arrived.
The grill is fired up again,
Reruns of syndicated stories are repeated,
A bottle has been presented.

"Hey, new guy!" I shout.
And the infinite cycle starts once more.
Under brilliant stars,
I watch a young man fall into a deep brandy-induced slumber.

I take the last tug at Napoleon.
As the bottle empties,
It is time to go home.

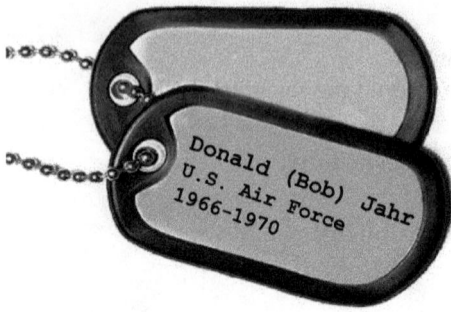

Donald (Bob) Jahr
U.S. Air Force
1966-1970

Donald (Bob) Jahr served in the U.S. Air Force from Oct. 6, 1966 until May 16, 1970. His MOS was 55151 Construction Equipment Operator. He served in Vietnam from Aug. 2, 1969 until May 15, 1970 attached to the 377th Combat Support Group. The VA did not originally have him listed as a Vietnam Veteran due to an administrative error. Luckily, Bob had saved all his records, including travel orders and MAC boarding passes, which helped him get everything straightened out by October of 1970, five months after his discharge.

The Clean-up Crew

Another plane gone down.
Better call out the clean-up crew.
Come on boys we got a job to do.
What happened here?
No one says.
No one asks.
And we need not know.
We're just the clean-up crew.

Come on boys this one's bad.
A road we have to build.
Just a tad.
The sun so bright.
The mood so dark.
Some made it out and they're all right.
Some did not and we'll treat them right.
Hero's all is their plight.
We're the clean-up crew.

Come on boys we got a job to do.
No leaves on the trees.
Mud up to our knees.
Pick up all the pieces big and small.
Don't leave a thing to tell the tale.
It all goes home before it's stale.
We're the clean-up crew.

Across the way friend or foe.
We do not know.
Black pajamas, round straw hats.
Rifles slung low.
We better go.
But rest assured we'll be back.
We got a job to do.
We're the clean-up crew.

The Letter

Staring at this page
My thoughts a jumble
What should I write
I seem to have stumbled

I started out
My thoughts clear as day
Then a cloud passed over
And it seems to have stayed

They long for a letter
So I will write
They want to hear
I'm all right

To write this letter
A few minutes it will take
A few minutes is all I can muster
A few minutes is all I can master
A few minutes to sooth their fears
A few minutes to make them feel better

How are you doing I hear them say
I'm doing fine is what they want to hear
I'm doing fine is what they need to hear
I'm doing fine is what I answer
In this hell hole I'm in
It's not a sin to tell a lie
Just some words to soothe the fears
Of the ones, I hold dear

By the time it arrives
How many more will have died
Will it be my time?
Will I be the next in line?

I stare at the page
And I begin to write
I'm doing fine
Having a grand time
I couldn't be better

Well, I have to go now
I'll write again real soon
Another lie
Till next time
Bye for now
Before it's my time

Michael Beesley
U.S. Army
2003-2011

Former Army Sergeant and current college student, Michael Lewis Beesley was born in the great state of Missouri in the early 80's. Life did not get better from there.

When not focused on his two wonderful children, Michael spends most of his time daydreaming between the infinite ocean of the What-If and the endless sky of the Could-Be-Was. Somewhere along the way, he might have lost his mind. If found, do not return. Dispose of it according to local hazardous material laws and pray for your sanity.

The Diagnosis

"Please, have a seat Mrs. Thompson." Dr. Roberts motioned to the chair opposite her desk. Mrs. Thompson stood in the doorway and looked around the room cautiously. The walls were decorated liberally. Dr. Roberts had hung several portraits of her family around the office, intermingled with her various degrees and certificates. Several pictures showed her son smiling at the camera with a happy, toothless grin. Dr. Roberts sat calmly at her desk with a matronly smile.

"Please, Mrs. Thompson. The sooner we begin, the sooner we can figure this out."

Clutching her purse tightly to her chest, Mrs. Thompson sighed before slowly lowering her rotund frame into the seat. Dr. Roberts shuffled some papers in front of her, sporadically checking notes on her desktop and making little clicking noises with her mouse.

"I have a referral here from your primary care physician and some lab results that he has sent me. I'd like to go over what has been happening before we decide on a next step. Can you tell me what brought you in to see the doctor?"

Mrs. Thompson shuffled in her seat. She looked down at the purse in her lap with sad eyes.

"I've already told this story to Dr. Geoffrey," she began, sheepishly.

"I know," Dr. Roberts reassured her. "I just want to make sure everything in his notes is correct. I want us to come up with the best plan for you."

Slowly but surely, Mrs. Thompson worked up the courage to explain what had been happening.

"It all started almost a year ago." She looked out the window, tears welling up in her eyes. "I was just feeling sick at first. Tired all the time. Some mornings I couldn't get out of bed until after noon." She looked down at her left hand and fiddled with her wedding ring. "It was the anniversary of Henry's passing. So, I thought I was just sad. I didn't think it was serious enough to see a doctor about."

Mrs. Thompson's eyes darted uncomfortably around the room. She couldn't look another person in the eyes while telling this story. Finally, her eyes rested again on her purse. She pulled out a tissue from inside and dabbed the corners of her eyes before continuing.

"Then... then I started having these... cravings. It was just for red meat, at first. Meatloaf, steak, just normal things. But it all tasted too done. Too cooked." Mrs. Thompson shifted. A crow outside cawed. "I cooked them rare, but it still wasn't enough. Some days I just warmed the meat on the skillet for a few minutes before I ate it. Then I started eating it raw."

Tears were falling down her cheeks now. She paused and stared at the pictures around the room. Her gaze never stayed long on the small boy, quickly moving along after recognizing the smile.

Dr. Roberts read over Dr. Geoffrey's notes. Everything so far was consistent with her expected diagnosis. There were just a few more details she needed to hear.

After letting Mrs. Thompson collect herself, she broke the silence. "Tell me about Jasper."

The poor woman broke down. Sobbing. "I didn't mean to. I didn't know what I was doing. That poor cat. I loved him."

Dr. Geoffrey's notes had gone into detail about this. At one point, several months ago. Mrs. Thompson picked up her cat, petted it leisurely, then took a bite out of it. The cat fought back, dealing massive scratches to Mrs. Thompson before she killed it and ate most of it. Paramedics, alerted by neighbors because of the loud noises, had found her wandering outside her apartment complex afterwards. She had been confused, bloodied, and lost.

"I told the doctors I didn't know what happened. I don't know why I did it. I was so hungry." She looked at the pictures in the room. Her eyes settled on the child again. He had such a grin on him. He was so young. So defenseless. It would be so easy... "Please, Doctor. I don't know what else I'm going to do. I need to know what's wrong with me. I'm always so hungry."

Dr. Roberts finished typing into her computer and looked at Mrs. Thompson. She sat up, straightened her lab coat, and looked Mrs. Thompson in the eye.

"Mrs. Thompson, we should probably run more tests, but I'm fairly certain you are technically deceased."

Mrs. Thompson buried her face in her hands. Dr. Geoffrey had gone over possible diagnoses before, this had been the one she dreaded most.

"Some time, a few years ago. You suffered a heart attack in your sleep but didn't pass away as usual. This condition isn't named yet and has been more and more prevalent in recent months. We don't understand much about it, but your symptoms of lethargy, kreatophagia, and your lack of vital signs align well with the diagnosis."

"We're lucky we caught it in time. Undiagnosed cases often lead to the development of an homnivorous appetite and uncontrollable exopahgy."

"I don't..."

Dr. Roberts pulled a folder from her desk and offered it to Mrs. Thompson.

"It's all explained in these pamphlets. We'll schedule more labs to confirm a diagnosis and we'll have another meeting in a month to view those results and discuss your prognosis. We also have a support group that meets weekly here in the hospital. Don't be worried. You can still lead a normal, fulfilling life. In fact, I've also been diagnosed with this condition, and I haven't had to curtail my practice at..."

The door burst open.

Corporal Diaz surveyed the room. Her weapon, an M14 rifle, was at the ready to shoot anything that moved. She held her breath and listened.

It was a doctor's private office. Faded pictures adorned the walls. Certificates and degrees showed that it belonged to Dr. Roberts. She was probably the body sprawled across the desk. It must have been sitting in here for some time. The skin was desiccated. Insects and scavengers didn't eat this kind of dead, so the body just sits there, for years.

In the other seat was another body. This had to be one of her patients. It was hanging half out of the chair, motionless.

Before the full measure of the plague was understood, the living didn't realize the infestation that was growing among them. The dead acted perfectly normal, except for… well, not dying. They continued getting up in the morning, going to work, and raising families.

The only difference was that they didn't heal like living people. A small scratch would never go away. It would also never get infected. Bacteria and viruses would never touch them.

It was months after the plague hit before anyone knew something was wrong. Some people didn't die, to the confusion of many doctors. Even then, they didn't do much about it. How could they know? If Grandpa didn't have a beating heart, but still acted like Grandpa, would you shoot him?

It wasn't until later, when the brains had withered away one cell at a time, that the true horror presented itself.

Corporal Diaz watched both corpses closely and exhaled slowly. The dead, in the absence of prey, continued the routines of their last days. They'd keep going until they finally collapsed where they were or sit down and never get back up. They still wouldn't be dead, or fully dead, just inert. They would be waiting patiently for prey to arrive. If their muscles still worked, that's when they would strike.

Who knew how long these two had been in this room?

She couldn't shoot them, yet. It was better to note the locations of any bodies and let the cleanup crews take care of them. They had to conserve ammunition.

"Bleach Six, this is Bleach Two-Three. Over." Their commander had thought it hilarious to steal their call signs from cleaning products.

"This is Bleach Six, go ahead."

"I've got two possible mobiles on the third floor, suite C. Rest of the floor is clear." She turned to exit the room.

"Good copy, see you at the entrance."

There was some shuffling behind her. She spun around to see the corpse from the chair standing up, arms stretched out to catch Corporal Diaz.

The corpse lunged at Corporal Diaz and Diaz brought the muzzle of her rifle up and into the corpse's face. A quick, three-round burst escaped the barrel, impacting the corpse and sending it backwards over the chair. Diaz quickly followed. Another three-round burst punctured the corpse's skull and it stopped moving.

There was no splatter. The skull had dried out long ago.

Corporal Diaz panted heavily, eyes and rifle fixed on the corpse. She quickly shifted focus to the other corpse on the desk. Luckily, it hadn't moved at all. Corporal Diaz took no chances and loosed a well-aimed round into that corpse, for good measure.

"This is Bleach two-three. As you were, there are no mobiles on the third floor. We still need cleaners."

"This is Bleach Six. Everything ok?"

"I'm green. Third floor is clear. I'll meet you downstairs."

Matthew Lee enlisted in the U.S. Navy in 2003 and graduated Master at Arms "A" School in 2004. Shortly after graduation, he was stationed in Guam with base security. In 2005 he volunteered for deployment to Cuba. In 2007 at the end of his enlistment he was awarded an honorable discharge, and moved to Missouri where he and his wife became published authors. They have two incredible kids Zayne and Katy. He enjoys pyrography and attending local comic-cons.

We All Bleed Blue

We all bleed blue
Believe that it's true
You can look at the science
If you so choose

We all bleed blue
That's what they said
The boot camp instructors
Who sit behind their desks

Skin or gender,
Creed or faith,
None of it matters
In the great debate,
For we are all Sailors
And we share the same fate.
For those who've never seen it
Surely you'd think it red
But that's a lie I tell you
It's really blue instead

On sand or snow,
On grass or dirt,
Doesn't matter where it falls
It will always hurt

First Bradley and Brant,
Carroll and Combs,
Just a few Sailors
Who never made it home

My brothers, my sisters
Who bled bluer
Than the deep blue sea
Spirits in my head
I fear them you see
They haunt my dreams
As if pulling me apart
At the very seams.

We all bleed blue.

John T. Grady II joined the Marine Reserves in 1994 as a food service supply clerk. In 1996 he evolved into a higher form of Marine life and joined the Navy Seabees as a Builder. He served for nine years in the Seabees performing construction and contingency construction on four continents. He served two deployments to Iraq in support of Operation Iraqi Freedom and provided disaster recovery assistance when Hurricane Katrina made landfall on the Mississippi Gulf Coast.

After Hurricane Katrina, he left the Seabees for the private sector to further expand his construction knowledge. He spent ten years developing and implementing new workflows, which brought advanced technology to the construction industry. He was instrumental in shaping construction standards for many government agencies. Today, he is the operation director for a local non-profit that serves veterans and people affected by cancer. He lives in Bay, Missouri with his wife Kara and two boys, Liam and Charles, along with a veritable zoo of animals.

Do Not Answer the Call

Forged and hardened in life a warrior emerges
Battles have raged both physical and mental
Honor is our guiding light
Yet the world has become devoid of honor

A sad sweetness calls
Offering promises of safety
Calm is offered in chaos
A light in a stormy sea

The seduction grabs a hold and twists us
Things we have done come to haunt us
The hereafter and its promise calls us
The pain and its strength shove us

A melody so appealing it can blind us
Reason is laid to rest as the lie engulfs us
The truth and world can be ugly
The siren veils the truth

Her sweetness calls lovingly for us
As we wrestle with the truth
Her melodies give a warm embrace
Yet that embrace hides the truth

We fight and resist her seductions
We need to rise again to battle against her call
Don't go off to the sweet sadness
Do not answer her call

Behind the Mask

What I once was, you knew well.
What I am now, I can't even tell.

I live in the darkness, Encased by fear.
A smile on my face, but it is only a mask my dear.

The mask engulfs me, we become one
How long 'til it's over when will it be done?

Darkness surrounds, the demons are near.
Strength it eludes me, I succumb to my fear.

Destruction of mind, destruction of soul
They whisper I'm crazy, but how can they know?

Death Will Find You

Our lives are an illusion
Deceived to think we are alive
We fear the dead and run from death.

Wherever you go, wherever hide
Death will always find you to take your life.

Through death we are reborn
Fear the dead no longer
Embrace death never mourn.

Twilight

As Sun wains,
Sister Moon shines bright.
Accompanied by,
the first star of night.
A point in spacetime,
where past, present, and future are in sight.

A timeless space,
where possibilities outnumber the stars.
A frightening place,
Where fears and worries are never far.
A joyous space,
Where memories and love flood our soul.

At that moment,
time suspended.
At that moment,
past, present, and future are one.
At that moment,
the majesty of the light of life is revealed.

Alien Country

An ideal. A promise. A Nation no more. I volunteered to defend the
Land of the Free. My family sacrificed time from me for the greater
good of that Nation. Yet never did we ever fathom what would
become of the Nation we loved. A Nation that stood above the rest
as a bastion for equality and liberty. Where has that Nation
gone? Did this happen overnight?

The sad answer is that terrorism is winning. Our liberties have
become more and more restrictive since that warm day in mid-
September 2001. A day that started out beautifully became darkened
by terror. The cloud that overshadowed our Nation has not
lifted. We live now in fear propagated by the media and our
government. We are asked to forego Constitutional Liberties in the
name of safety. There was a bright spot when we as a Nation came
together to heal but it was only superficial as days later the Nation
became divided once again. Although this time the division became
ugly. It became us and them. It didn't matter if you disagreed. No
longer was there discourse. No longer was there debate. Vitriol and
fear filled our Nation.

Many of us answered the call to defend our Nation and our way of
life. Yet that many compared to the populous was and is negligible.
The Nation no longer sacrifices along with those who defend
her. The Nation, eager to send those defenders into harm's way, is
more comfortable observing through the television. Oh yes there are
parades, discounts, and support our troops ribbons. Yet there are
veterans on the streets. Veterans are suffering. Veterans are dying.
Veterans are forgotten.

The burden of the Nation and of the world is placed on their
shoulders to bare. Yet few share in their suffering and sacrifice.
Even presidential candidates show their ignorance of these
sacrifices. Some have gone as far as saying they always wanted a
Purple Heart. Not understanding the suffering, bad days, and
nightmares that come with that award. The Nation no longer

recoils in outrage at these statements as the Nation no longer sacrifices and expects these few men and women along with their families to share the burden alone.

The Nation has become a glutton of microwave thinking. It happens now and they forget about it five minutes later. The news no longer cares that men and women are called to fight all over the globe. Half of the population couldn't identify most of the locations our military deploys to. The Nation no longer has skin in the game.

Is this the year America dies? We have a Neo-Fascist running against a Neo-Communist in the two main stream parties. We see a Nation more at ease with party loyalties and talking points than they are with the Constitution. The Constitution is our foundation and it has been chipped away where only a few corner stones are present. How soon till those stones are toppled? I have become an alien in my own country.

William (Bill) Tracy was born on September 19, 1974. His father served in the U.S. Army and was stationed in Germany during the Vietnam War. In the spring of 1992 he enlisted and was sworn into the U.S. Army as a 13-B Heavy Artillery Crewmember. His father had to sign William's enlistment papers as he was only 17 and needed parental consent. He attended Basic and Advanced Training at Fort Sill, Oklahoma.

In 1993, while lifting artillery rounds, William slipped and his ankle got caught in the ammunition rack. He finished his two-year service, but unfortunately the surgery and injury barred him from reenlistment for medical reasons.

William went on to graduate Cum Laude with a BA in English from combined studies at Missouri STL and the Pierre Laclede Honors College.

He currently lives in Warrenton, Missouri and is a Postal Clerk for the town of Morrison, Missouri.

Superman

I am not Superman.
I was raised to believe in Truth,
Justice,
And the American way.

As I age, I am told truth is subjective.
Justice, no longer exists.
And the American Way is racist and bigoted.

I strive to help my fellow man.
Even when they do not deserve it,
And despite their faults.

I have my kryptonite,
I keep believing in others,
Even when they hurt me and hurt me.

I can't fly, but my spirit wants to soar.
I want to see new worlds of adventure.

You can feel the heat in my eyes,
The truth in my words.

My words at times can leave you frozen to the core with a breath.
My mind races along like a speeding train.
My imagination can clear the tallest of buildings.

I am not Superman.
But I strive to be.

There is Beauty in the Winter

Snow covers the world in a blanket of white
It seems that nature dies

Trees bereft of leaves
Flowers have lost their beauty
All looks forlorn and forgotten

But there is a profound quiet peace in the silent desolation
And from that peace
Spring will come anew

We know this to be an unending truth
Flowers will bloom
Trees will regain their splendor

Renewal is coming
A new dawn will break
If we but have the patience to wait

Sing to me spring
Bring forth revival
Allow my soul to flourish
And go into the eternal summer to which we all deserve

Last Night's Dream

I had a dream last night.
There was a large crowd of beautiful people,
Dressed in beautiful costumes and regalia.
The kind you see at a Mardi Gras parade.

This crowd made me happy.
My spirit wanted to join them in their reverie.
I rose to float above the crowd,
Looking at their smiling beatific faces.

I hovered above watching,
But never fully joining in the festivity.

I saw a face who's beauty struck to my core.
I knew I must follow and perhaps,
Join as soon as I was able.

They began to move in a wondrous dance,
Marching through the doors,
Into winding corridors of a spectacular building.

I flew along in such joy.
I love to fly,
And in flying I was with them.

But their dance gained speed.
I began to fall behind,
Losing them in the winding way of halls and doors.

I searched.
Sadness began as I could not seem to find them.
But I felt I was close.
Suddenly I felt pulled to the earth,
By some weighty hand.

It was a shadow.
It pulled me down,
Holding me tight against the floor.

It was a shadow of my past.
It was trying to keep me from flying,
From finding the wondrous future.

I knew without a doubt,
The shadow could not last in the light of the day.

I began to search,
Search for a way out of the building,
An exit or something leading to the outside.

I saw a door off to the side.
I opened it pulling the shadow along,
Dragging slowly across the floor.

As the door opened,
I first saw a window,
The light blazing just outside its pane.

I knew if I could only get it open,
The light would blaze inside,
And I would be free to fly once again.

Then I noticed the room was full of debris,
A room of pain and torture.

I had to cross,
It was the only way to free my soul.
I walked,
Painfully, Slowly,
Through glass, needles, pins,

A vast array of torturous objects.
Feeling my feet rip, cut, bleed with every step.
Still onward I strode,
Pushing through the anguish,
My goal was in sight,
My spirit pushed me onward.

After a slow painful walk,
With my feet bleeding and raw,
I reached the window.

I smiled and lifted the pane.
On the other side I sighed.
Another pane of glass.
I once again reached and opened.

And there was another.
I opened pane after pane,
Waiting to see the light flow through.
Never stopping,
Sometimes having to work at the lock,
Or struggling to open the window.
Once even having to smash through,
Leaving my hands as bloodied as my poor feet.

Then I woke from this dream,
Stoic and strong.
I did not reach the light last night,
But the window is still there,
And it will be opened.

Perhaps in another dream.

Pop-Tarts and Ports

Friends, colleagues, geeks, and nerds
I am here to welcome you to the First Holy Communion of
        Pop-Tarts and Port
We share wondrous revelations with you who are gathered
        here today
We have discovered that the interpretation of a portion of
        the Good Book was wrong
The meek shall not inherit the Earth
It is the geek who shall inherit the Earth
One little letter and all things change
Brethren our time is now and the Kingdom is here
No more swirlies for quoting Tolkien
Now we have Viggo Mortensen
And he rallies the ghosts of the ancients and geeks can follow
        behind
No more hiding in the bathroom stall to read the works of
        the great Stan Lee
Now his memory is celebrated by both jocks and nerds
        alike Excelsior
No more hiding in our parent's basements playing the games
        of Jackson and Gygax
Now we can see the imaginations of those great men on
        computer and movie screens
Mutant and man, jock and nerd all celebrate the wonder that
        is the geek
Wafers and wine are now replaced by Pop-Tarts and port
And Jesus can be a lumberjack as well as a Middle Eastern hippy
Bow your heads and give thanks to the wonder of an all
        knowing and powerful deity
Who celebrates with us today in our geekiness and joy
Our time has come
Our place is here
We are united and the world is ours

We create

Our images, our passions, our dreams have taken the Earth and
we rejoice in the communion of all

I leave you my friends with these words of wisdom from our
forefathers:

Live long and prosper and Nanu Nanu

Jon Freeland was born in Bethesda, Maryland and lived several places early as a Navy brat before settling in Jefferson City, Missouri. Jon's father served in the U.S. Navy for eleven years.

Jon works as a systems consultant and relationship coach to agencies within the Division of Developmental Disabilities as well as a part-time Luthier. He wrote poetry as an English major in college and has really come into his muse since March 2018. He's been reading monthly with the community at Belle Book & Candle, featured at the bi-weekly Belle Ringer open mic, and presented with select poets in the recent Osage Arts Community program to honor returning alumnus Jason Baldinger.

O! Vigil, ante hero—
Of Vicky, Alan, John, and Edgar
(A WWI Inspired Poem)

easily studied,
for stones and sentinels cannot move.
They are photographs without film—
slumbering hearts fore shuddered
in hope of another great awakening—
evermorely waiting for my whim.
I. The Silverwhelming,

And he, dressed olive green,
at attention for imagined peace
equipped with the branch
that grows from his brambled hand;

his rigor has never failed
this eternal bunker, walled
off from outside invasion
but slowly falling to infestation

such as that which he sustained young,
when he had no need for home
and sung of Victory while they pinned
the metals to his vest where they lay him down to rest.

Then he made good his first promise,
drinking the last laudanum,
feeding the birds so they
may fight in his dead.

This other one carries the cross,
    red and white and red
sweat and bled for the lost
    of leg, arm, and head.

They once were green, but Autumn meddled
yellow, orange, red and settled
   my hand upon the maple leaf and pressed
   against the veins now gray, distressed
wild infants crying in field cradles,
   addled before even time could test.

The last soldier was a precious pretender, no fighter,
never allowed to be a lover. Is there such a wonder
as the villainy of a heart – treacherous and still – laid over
lapel and exposed in each beat for Life to plunder?

They say the Victor writes the history;
is Death betrayed by breathing hands?
What hubris have the living to understand
what they bury in a box labeled "mystery?"

….

In ebon twilence, I pour us a glass
and reverently lay down upon the old ground
with three simple roses for three loves misplaced.
That is where I found waiting for me
willing for me
pleading for me
REACHING FOR ME.

I cannot be satiated on their redeeming graces—
They're screaming inside their smiling faces—
I'M SCREAMING inside my innermost sanctum!
If only I had simply come here and thanked them
and left and lived in sweet unknowing—

Now I wander in search of the source of the crowing.

Reverie

"Taps, taps, lights out! All hands turn into your bunks!
Maintain silence about the decks!
The smoking lamp is out in all berthing spaces!"

To remind him of the worst,
Paul's flesh had a thorn;
my big toe has a boil on it,
and it hurts.

At sea, they called it "Liberty,"
with a warning:

"Lights out is 21:00.
I don't care what you do when you're dreamin',
just keep your hands to yourself,
don't touch the water,
and don't do anything on your own.

Otherwise, a Master-at-Arms
will put a boot on your chest
and crawl so far up your ass,
he can see daylight through your throat.

That goes double for going home.
Avoid crowds, don't drink, don't babysit alone."

The medical corpsman watched him eager to come clean,
a dollop of care in Barbasol cream.
Six month tours are never the same;
some things a man carries are heavier than planes.

When a sick bay phone call suffocated the night,
I cursed and wiped the innocence from my eyes:
"Madson, what in God's green earth is going on?"
"Petty officer, I need a favor. I think something's wrong."
We both knew better what it's like to miss your children
but spend your life solving the problems of grown men.

"Call 911," I confess in clueless therapy.
This sore is the stain of all the roads that used to be.

The infection spreads as I lay in my room:
"Reveille, Reveille, all hands on deck!
All sweepers man your brooms!"

Jason Mayer joined the Marine Corps in 1992 and served for eight years as a Combat Correspondent covering stories on five continents and more than 50 countries. During the later years of his military career, he transitioned from working as a reporter and press chief with newspapers and took on more public affairs related tasks including public relations and media relations.

After leaving the Marine Corps, he spent eight years working with government contractors supervising the development of more than 200 annual publishing projects. Today, he is a partner in a construction company that designs and builds playgrounds and recreational areas.

Jason holds bachelor's degrees in Communications and Business Management and an MBA from the University of Maryland. He also holds a PhD in Public Policy and Administration from the University of Maryland, Baltimore County. He lives in Columbia, Missouri with his wife Angela and two boys, Noah and Caleb.

The Creative Process

As a military reporter and public affairs specialist, Jason wrote hundreds of press releases and news articles. While always factual, these pieces normally went through vetting processes that left the final versions very sterilized, redacted, and often devoid of emotional details. As a counter measure, Jason would often write narrative poems as an emotional release. The following is a collection of packaged press releases and poems showcasing this creative process.

Flight Jacket

Vol. 2, No. 18   Sept. 29, 2000

Proud Sponsor of cheesy beef jerky, chocolate milk and all food made of 'crap'

Good night Bat Boy, where ever you are

By Patrick Michael Brandon
"Moonshine" Cetus

Well whooopdeedoo!!

"I miss deff cherdesst Mayes.
He was my diggest dan."

Bat Boy,
Drinking buddy,
long-time admirer

His 'chumming' technique was unorthodox, yet strangely effective

Sept. 29, 2000 *Flight Jacket* Page 1

DATELINE: YUMA, AZ, NOVEMBER 6, 1995 – A Marine based at Marine Corps Air Station Yuma was found dead at his residence in base housing yesterday morning. Military police and medical personnel were called to the scene where his death was ruled a suicide as the result of a self-inflicted gunshot wound.

The name of the Marine is being withheld pending notification of next of kin. An investigation is ongoing and more information will be released as it becomes available.

Officer of the Day

Officer of the Day
It's a boring duty
Especially on Sunday
Slow and dull
24 hours of mindless trudging
A few odd phone calls
Driving around base to rattle locked doors
New arrivals to check-in
Lots of solitaire
A bit of light reading
Long meals at the chow hall to pass the time

Today's Officer of the Day is a second lieutenant
Just a butter bar, four months out of OCS
He started the day bright-eyed and bushy tailed
21 hours later his eyes are much dimmer
The monotony of routine has sapped his focus

It's now 4 a.m., dark and quiet
He grabs a quick nap at the desk
A loud ring startles him
Grabbing the phone he answers professionally
A second ring startles him even more
He had grabbed the wrong phone
The tan phone is for general business
The red phone is for emergencies
The red phone never rings
But it is ringing now

The young lieutenant picks it up
It's the Military Police Dispatch
Shots fired
Units at the scene
Officer of the Day needed at Base Housing
No further details, just hurry

The young lieutenant grabs his cover and calls for his driver
Base housing is only five minutes away
Just long enough to speculate
Was it a fight
A crazy party
Domestic violence
Probably something like that

The driver turns into the area
A lone police car is parked in the street
Emergency lights still flashing

The Officer of the Day approaches the scene
Looking for answers
A burly sergeant meets him at the door
His face is pale, his eyes glassy
He snaps a salute and grunts out the facts

Call came in at zero three forty five
Shots fired at this unit
One dead on arrival,
One dependent child on location,
Scene still being secured
NCIS has been notified
Sergeant of the Guard is inside

The lieutenant nods and walks toward the door
Sir, you better prepare yourself.
Another nod and a few more steps toward the door

A pool of blood at the threshold causes him to stop
He pushes his head through the opening
He can see a staircase
A limp body lays across the bottom steps
Blood and debris splattered on the wall

The body is that of a man
A tall man wearing his Class A uniform
Gun dropped next to an open right hand
Eyes closed, mouth open
Large hole in his head

The lieutenant wretches but holds it in
He stares a bit longer in disbelief
Then he hears a sound
Feels a presence
He turns his head and sees a little boy

The young lieutenant has been trained for war
Prepared for bullets, bombs and blood
But he has not been trained for this
To see a five-year-old boy
Sitting in a puddle of piss and tears

A small human standing only feet away from his dead father
His hands clasped over his ears
Pushing hard to block out the world
His mouth hung open in a silent scream
Goosebumps raised on his cold little arms
Scooby Doo PJs covered in blood and filth
Tiny toes curled on bare feet trying to avoid the sticky floor

The Captain of the Guard appears from the hallway
Wraps the boy in a blanket
Picks him up in strong arms
Carries him way from the horror

Passing by the lieutenant he shakes his head
There's nothing more to see in there, son
Best you get on with it

The Officer of the Day closes his eyes
Pulls in a deep breath
Spins around to face the world
He turns to face a new challenge
A pretty brunette has arrived
She rushes at the door

The young lieutenant blocks her way
She can still see the horror
She explodes into hysterics
Crying and screaming incoherently
Only a few words can be discerned

Divorce,
Cheating,
Bastard,
Hate,
Betrayal,
Why,
Coward,
Selfish,
Where is my son!

The Captain of the Guard stops
Hands the swaddled boy to an officer
Grabs the hysterical lady
Guides her away from the house
Away from the chaos

The Officer of the Day looks at him pleadingly
What do I do, Captain
Call everyone, son
Just call everyone

Finding his bearing, he locates his duty log
There is a list of names
He calls them all

Commanding General notified
Commanding Officer notified
Sergeant Major notified
Chaplain notified
Family Services notified
Public Affairs notified
Determine next of kin

Who the hell is the next of kin?

The traumatized 5-year-old?
The hysterical ex-wife?
The man had to have parents
Let's go with that

The chaplain arrives first
Thank the Lord
He takes charge of the drama
Consoles the inconsolable

Next is the Sergeant Major
Then Family Services
Before long everyone has arrived
A group of chiefs
But no one wants to lead this mission

The crowd is comforting to the young lieutenant
It is their responsibility now
He makes a few entries in his log

Signals his driver and exits the scene

As the sun peeks above the horizon
The Officer of the Day returns to his duty desk
Only one hour left

He tries to process all that has happened
But the process is maddening

They say no one has the right to judge another
But there are times when judgment must be made
Judgments about actions
Judgments about character
Judgment of the putrid affect others can have on the world

Seeing the five-year-old boy huddled on the floor,
The young lieutenant had made a judgment
A judgment to hate

To hate a man who was no longer a father
He had blown that right out the side of his head

A man who was no longer a husband
He had cheated away that right

A man who had become a monster
Some may call him a sick monster
A diseased monster
A monster broken by the hardships of the world
But those just excuses

The monster had the right to take his life
To end his misery
To leave this world in a bloody heap

But not in front of the boy
An innocent five-year-old

No man has that right
No human has that right
Not even a monster has that right
That is not his judgment
That is just a fact

It is zero eight hundred hours
His duty is over

The young lieutenant is no longer the Officer of the Day
Now he is just a butter bar again

DATELINE: NAIROBI, KENYA, MARCH 30, 1998 – Service
members from Marine Corps Air Station El Toro,
California recently participated in Operation Noble
Response a joint humanitarian mission launched in
response to the widespread flooding that has ravaged
several provinces in Kenya. Two KC-130 aircraft and
34 personnel from Marine Aerial Refueler Transport
Squadron 352 were deployed to the area after the
country experienced the greatest human and material
losses in the region's history.

According to the Kenyan government, more than 45
people have been found dead and several hundred are
still missing. Nearly 300,000 Kenyans have been
displaced from their homes and are suffering due to
lack of food and potable water. Farmland, livestock,
and food storages in the region have been compromised
by polluted flood water and rampant raiding by tribal
warlords. The flood waters have also caused the
collapse of more than 9,000 houses, as well as
hundreds of bridges, road systems, and other vital
infrastructure.

During the 60 day operation, Marines with the VMGR-
352 Raiders coordinated with the United Nations World
Food Program to deliver nearly two million pounds of
food via multiple air drops of food and water
throughout the region.

Chaos in Kenya

<u>PART 1</u>

15 minutes from the airfield
The KC-130 Hercules pitches
Leaning hard to the right
The aircraft dips down
Making a sharp U-turn
We are hundreds of miles from the coast
But a sea of dirty water lies below
Flooding as far as the horizon

The cargo plane levels out
Engines purring as they slow
Red light snaps on
Wiry corporal bounces out from the cockpit

Time to do the Lord's work boys
Let's feed the masses

The jovial loadmaster heads for the payload
He loosens the ratchet straps
Whistling while he works
Large pallets move on steel rollers
Flats full of rice, grain, and bottled water

The corporal slaps a yellow button
An alarm rings out
Belly of the plane yawns open
Sun is blinding as it rushes in
Plastic wrapped pallets glisten

Hook up boys
Time to push

Two other Marines join the party
All three are in gray flight suits
Fitted with orange harnesses
They hook up to rope lines
All in the name of safety
No one wants to fall out

They stand behind the last pallet
Pushing hard and grunting
The line begins to move
Six large flats in all

They build up speed
Cargo nears the edge
First pallet launches into the air
Second follows fast
Then the third and fourth

Each release causing the plane to bounce
Just a couple inches every time

The fifth one gets caught
A hefty shove breaks it loose
Then out goes five and six

The loadmaster clicks the intercom
Payload is free
The pilot acknowledges
Red light flickers off

Three Marines stand at the rear
Leaning against their ropes
Staring at the dirty water below

PART 2

The cargo tumbles down
Crashing into heaps

Bounty for the hungry
Flood ravaged locals
Dying of starvation
Waiting… hoping for relief

They stare for a moment
A loud BANG rings out

Then they see it
A black 'mech
An old beat up Ford Ranger
Fitted with a 50 Caliber machine gun
Manned by a small crew

The Marines' eyes widen
Loadmaster springs into action
He hits the yellow button
An alarm rings out
The belly starts to close

BANG!
BANG!
BANG!
BANG!

GET TO THE CENTER!
GET TO THE CENTER!
GET TO THE CENTER!
GET... TO... THE... CENTER!

The three Marines dive
Landing hard on the rollers

Loud bangs continue to ring
Now louder and faster

The gunner has found his mark
Bullets cut through the metal side

Small holes appear at random
Sun rays shine through the top and side
Louder clangs are heard from below
Thank God for the armored belly

The aircraft pulls up sharply
The men slide backward on rollers
Rope lines pulling tight
Harnesses holding everyone in place

An explosion is heard from the right
Plane rocks to the left
Smoke
Then fire
One engine down

Don't panic! Yells the corporal
We still have three more

Another round of bangs
The gunner has reloaded

The sound gets louder
Again, he has found his mark
Another line of holes
A second explosion
This one to the left
The plane rocks right

Smoke
Then fire
Two engines down

The men huddle in the center
Holding tight to the steel rollers

Next comes thudding sounds
CHUNK, CHUNK, CHUNK, CHUNK
Followed by loud pops
Then crackling noises

The loadmaster smiles
We are popping flares
That should blind the bastards

PART 3

The banging has stopped
But no one moves
Hearts pounding
Ears ringing
Waiting for death

You boys okay back there?
The pilot's voice is jarring
We should be out of range now

We are good
The corporal slowly stands
Just bumps and bruises
The other two stand
Checking themselves for holes

It's the pilot again
Better strap in
Might get hairy
Engines one and three are out
And four is limping
But engine two is humming along

The loadmaster buckles up fast
Until now he had been calm
The other Marines follow suit

Buckles tight
Prayers said
Heads tucked
Eyes closed
Tray tables up
Ready for landing
Crash or otherwise

The remaining engines growl
Struggling to carry the giant bird
Laboring hard
But still running

Ten long minutes pass
The Hercules slows
Then drops quickly
Stomachs lurch
Eyes close

White knuckles grip tight
Everyone holds their breath
The landing is bumpy
Then a hard stop
Thank the Lord
Everyone is alive

The pilot steps out
He is all smiles
It's all good boys
Let's slap on some new engines
We got more runs tomorrow

DATELINE: BANGKOK, THAILAND, MAY 16, 1996 – The Armed Forces of the United States and Thailand conducted the 15th Exercise Cobra Gold at various locations throughout the Kingdom of Thailand May 2-14.

Cobra Gold is one of the largest theater security exercises in the Indo-Pacific and is an integral part of America's commitment to strengthen relationships in the region.

The objective of the exercise is to improve the capabilities of participating nations to plan and conduct combined and joint operations; build relationships among participating nations; and improve interoperability over a range of activities.

This year's exercise was attended by 29 countries either directly participating in or observing Cobra Gold 96, including approximately 4,500 U.S. personnel both ashore and afloat.

Thai Press Chief: Day One

The first bar was too dark
Second was too loud
Third one is perfect

The Bangkok Inn has great lighting
No live bands
Plenty of tables
Room for rent upstairs
Two dozen pretty girls

At only 10 a.m.
I grab a corner booth
It has a power outlet
Pay phone within reach
Two large windows
Good access to the head
Sits opposite the main bar
Taxi stand at the entrance
Food market next door
One hour photo across the street
This will make a solid home

I plop down my Mac Classic 2
Set up the keyboard
Set up the mouse
Disc in the drive
Pull out the assignment folders
Unfold a map
Ready for business

The house matron walks over
She looks confused
"What you doing?"

I show her my press badge
I'll be working here
Ten days
Lots of customers

She nods in agreement
You want girl
Yes! I want two
Two of your largest girls
Not top earners
Quiet girls who understand English

She nods and waves toward the bar
Two girls walk over
One could be described as burly
She will do
The other is thin but tall
Very tall
Might not even be a girl
Either way, she will do

I nod
Then hand the matron twenty dollars, American
Two fives for each bar fine
Ten for the booth rental
The matron smiles and walks away

I turn to the girls and bark out orders
I will be working here
People will come to the table
I will talk to them
Business only
No hookers
No waitresses
No buy-me-drinkies
No flower girls
No pictures

No bug baskets
No vendors
Only you two
I don't want to be bothered

You no sex? Asks the burly one
Me no sex
She looks disappointed
I know it's not because I'm so damn pretty
She thinks she's not getting paid

What's your name?
Malee.
Don't worry, Malee
You will make plenty of money
She looks confused
I hand her twenty bucks
Go buy a cooler
A twelve pack of Coke
Two bags of chips
Keep the change

I turn to the tall girl
What is your name?
Solada.
Still probably not a girl
Still doesn't matter
I hand Solada a twenty
Then four cans of film
Take these to a one-hour photo
Keep the change

With the girls on assignment
I pull some cardboard out of my bag
Grab some tape
Then slap a sign on the door
The PRESS OFFICE is now open at the Bangkok Inn

I sit down
Type out a quick story
Kick back and shut my eyes

At noon the first wave rolls in
Cobra Gold is a multi-national training exercise
It lasts 10 days
Runs throughout Thailand
Troops come in from all different countries
All different branches
Thousands of military
Dozens of civilians
Hundreds of prostitutes

I am expecting five reporters
A Petty Officer
An Airman
A Brit
An Aussie
And a Kiwi

The Sailor is the first to arrive
A large fellow with bulging arms
He ignores the girls and heads to the table
All business
I hand him his assignment folder
Two cans of film
Point to the map
Find the admiral
Get the scoop
Deadline is Fifteen Hundred Hours

Next is the Airman
A pretty young lady
She smiles at the girls
Then bounces my way
Now this is a nice office

I nod and smile
Then hand her a folder
Two Cans of Film
Point to the map
Find the general
Get the scoop
Deadline is Fifteen Hundred Hours

The Aussie and the Kiwi arrive together
Two giant men
They walk straight to the bar
The girls swoon
Eventually, they make their way to the table
I hand them their folders
Four cans of film
Point to the map
Find the front line
Get the scoop
Deadline is Fifteen Hundred Hours

The Brit is last
A thin proper lad
Impeccably dressed
He strides to the table
I hand him a folder
Two cans of film
Point to the map
Find the Thai Army
Get the scoop
Deadline is Fifteen Hundred Hours

The assignments have been doled out
I grab a Coke
Open a bag of chips
Bang out another story
Then kick back and shut my eyes

Three hours later the Airman returns
It's thirteen hundred hours
She hands me her notes
Two cans of film
Dictates her lead
Dictates her bridge
Reads off some quotes
I type it all in
Edit it twice
Nod my approval
Wave to Malee
First beer's on me

Thirty minutes later it's the Aussie and Kiwi
It's thirteen thirty hours
I start with the Aussie
The Kiwi waits impatiently
He hands me his notes
Two cans of film
Dictates his lead
Dictates his bridge
Reads off some quotes
I type it all in
Edit it twice
Nod my approval
Wave to Malee
First beer's on me

Now for the Kiwi
He repeats the process
Two cans of film
Lead, bridge, quotes
I edit it twice
I nod my approval
Wave to Malee
First beer's on me

The Sailor lumbers in
It's fourteen hundred hours
He hands me his notes, film, lead, bridge
Yada, yada
Edit it twice
Nod my approval
Wave to Malee
First beer's on me

The Brit is last
It's fourteen forty-five
Fifteen minutes to deadline
He hands me his notes
Two cans of film
Dictates his lead
Dictates his bridge
No time for quotes
I type it all in
Edit it once
And head to the phone

I call the office
Thank God it's Mary
She types like the wind
I read off the stories
Twenty minutes later
Seven stories filed

I plop back in my chair
Point to Malee
Get the Brit a beer
Get me two

I hand the bag of film to Solada
Along with fifty bucks
Take this to a one hour photo
Keep the change
I turn off the computer
Slam down a cold beer
Look over the crowd
Nearly a hundred strong
Equal parts native and foreign

The Airman has found a new friend
The Sailor is arm wrestling the Kiwi
The Aussie is heading up stairs for some fun

The Brit is reading a book
Not a bad day at the office

Only nine more days to go
Sixty-three stories
126 cans of film
And a lot more beer at the Bangkok Inn

I give ten dollars to Malee
Another ten to Solada
See you tomorrow girls

DATELINE: SAN DIEGO, CA, DECEMBER 10, 1999 – Six Marines and one Sailor assigned to the 15th Marine Expeditionary Unit were reported lost at sea Thursday after a Marine Corps helicopter crashed while ferrying troops between ships 14 miles off Point Loma.

Of the 18 service members aboard the CH-46 Sea Knight, 11 were rescued from the water just minutes after the early afternoon crash, which occurred as the craft took off from the amphibious assault ship Bonhomme Richard on its way to the oiler Pecos.

Despite using divers, helicopters and ships, a combined rescue effort by the Navy and Coast Guard failed to find any sign of the other six Marines, one Navy Petty Officer, or the 23,000-pound helicopter.

Of the 11 Marines rescued from the water, two were taken by air to the Balboa Naval Hospital in San Diego, where their injuries were described as minor. The other nine were treated aboard the Bonhomme Richard. No names of the injured or the missing have been released pending notification of next of kin.

The CH-46 was on a training exercise with ships and troops preparing for a six-month assignment, to begin next month in the Persian Gulf as part of the Bonhomme Richard Amphibious Ready Group.

The cause of the crash is still under investigation.

December 9, 1999
GySgt. James P. Paige, JR, Middlesex, NJ / Crew Chief
SSgt. Vincent A. Sabasteanski, Cumberland ME / Force RECON
SSgt. David E. Galloway, Oregon City, OR / Force RECON
SSgt. Jeffry R. Starling, South Dayton, FL / Force RECON
SSgt. William C. Dame, Yuma, AZ / Force Recon / EOD
Petty Officer Jay J. Asis, Quezon City, Philippines / Force RECON
Cpl. Mark A Baca, Jefferson City, MO / Force RECON

I am Not Allowed to Cry

Seven men died today
But I am not allowed to cry

I must tell their story
So I am not allowed to cry

A Sea Knight plunged into the ocean
Then sank into that dark Pacific

The press release is all but written
I must be clear, concise, specific

Just a training exercise I am forced to say
But no one ever trains to die

Just an accident, I tell the press
But even the truth sounds like a lie

Eighteen men on board
Seven lost souls
Eleven survivors
Nine with scratches
One broken leg
One lacerated liver

Seven men died today
But I am not allowed to cry

Six Marines and a Sailor died today
But I am not allowed to cry

It started on the Bonhomme Richard
A proud Amphibious Assault Ship

Then a short flight along the coast
A nice sunny day for a trip

On the Pecos the helo tried to land
But the rear wheel caught some netting

A tool meant to save
Became an instrument of death

Seven men died today
But I am not allowed to cry

Six Recon warriors and a crew chief died today
But I am not allowed to cry

Navy SEALS dove right in
Plucking men from the cold, blue water

Survivors found salvation through the Hell Hole
A thirty-four inch opening in the floor

Most were thrown far and wide
Mercy knocking them unconscious

For seven, the suction was too strong
And they were dragged to soggy graves

Seven men died today
But I am not allowed to cry

At 1316 hours they died today
But I am not allowed to cry

We gathered at the command center
Just waiting on the names

The families gathered far behind us
Just waiting on the names

The colonel shuffled through the door
His face pale, his head hung low

With closed eyes he recited the names
But only the command group could hear

Six were married
One engaged
Five were fathers
All of them brave

Ten children without dads
Five wives now widows
One fiancée without a groom
Many parents had lost a son

Seven men died today
But I am not allowed to cry

Seven families to be notified today
But I am not allowed to cry

I sat alone in a metal chair
And forced myself to watch

The wives
The children
The fathers
The mothers
Brothers
Sisters
Cousins
Friends
Neighbors
The colonel and chaplain approached the families
Too many to separate them all

The room was silent and sullen
The colonel cleared his throat and spoke

He started with the survivors
Each name met with cries of joy

He paused for an unbearable moment
Then named the lost

Each name, a broken home
Each name, a cry of pain

Every family reacted
Every reaction unbearable
Every cry a shot to the heart

The last name was called
Gunnery Sergeant James Paige Junior
He was my friend

Gunny Paige died today
But I am not allowed to cry

My friend Jimmy died today
But I am not allowed to cry

Jimmy was the first to surface
But he dove under to save more men

He led three Marines to freedom
But could not find his own way home

The general awarded Jimmy a medal
But it did little to ease the pain

His daughter Annalee would agree
So would Marianne his lovely wife

Seven men died today
But I am not allowed to cry

Six strangers and my friend died today
But I am not allowed to cry

The hunt for bodies went on for days
The water too cold to survive

Eventually the bodies were found
Scooped up by a small submarine

The memorial was held eleven days later
But the loss still did not feel real

At 1316 hours they read the names
The reactions were the same

Each name, a broken home
Each name, a cry of pain

Every family reacted
Every reaction unbearable
Every cry a shot to the heart

Amazing Grace was played
One fatherless child yelled *goodbye*

The colonel turned to us with watery eyes
"Okay Marines, let your tears flow"

Sorry Sir, I am forced to say,
I have no more tears left to cry

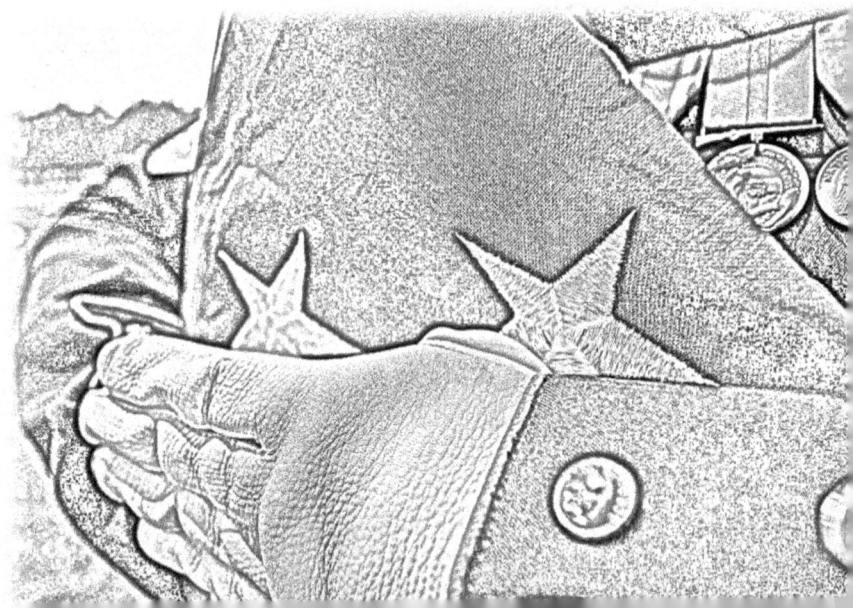

← 11番線　今度の電車　Next Departure

開車 時刻	列車名 Train Name	番号 Train No.	行先 Destination	記事 Remarks
7:34	はやぶさ・こまち	45号	新青森・秋田	こまち全車指定席

停車駅　こまち　　盛岡・田沢湖・角館・大曲・秋田

| 8:01 | やまびこ | 41号 | 盛岡 | 自由席1～3号車 |

停車駅　古川・くりこま高原・一ノ関・水沢江刺・北上・新花巻・盛岡

| 8:49 | はやぶさ | 101号 | 盛岡 | 全車指定席 |

の車内販売は東京～新青森駅、こまち号の車内販売

7:1

Last Train to Hiroshima

Staring at the large sign at the Tokyo train station,
I break into a cold sweat.
It's all Greek to me.
Well Kanji, I think that's what they call it.
I frantically try to match the hieroglyphics,
But the symbols on my ticket can't be found on the board.

A Japanese business man takes pity on me.
Where you going.
Hiroshima.
Other side, he says, pointing at the gaggle of travelers on the other
side of the tracks.
I shoot him a look of confusion.

Upstairs, over bridge, he says nodding wildly.
Panic flashes in my eyes.
The man smiles knowingly.
Must hurry! Last train leaves five minutes.

Danke schön! I shout as I run away.
My brain informs me that was German,
But it's too late to make a correction.

I race up the stairs;
Frightening Japanese families along the way.
Women press against the wall.
Mothers pull their children back for protection.
Men look up at me with scrunched up faces.

The scene is chaotic.
Six-two Marine.
Class A uniform.
Giant sea bag on back.
Forehead glistening with sweat.

I run wildly up the stairs,
Wide-eyed and frantic.

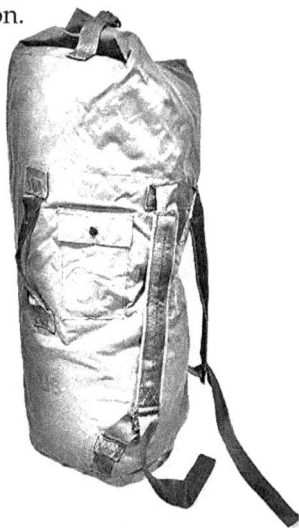

My height towers above the locals.
All eyes on the ugly American.
I feel guilty for scaring the children.
But half of them are giggling at the white giant,
So screw 'em.

Mercy be, the bridge is clear.
I sprint the 50 yards in record time.
Then make a left to head down the stairs.

An old Japanese lady screams as I nearly bowl into her.
I swerve quickly,
But the sea bag clips her shoulder.
Stupid Gai-jin! She shouts.
Sorry, Pardon, Lo Siento, I offer as I continue downward.

The parlay has compromised my balance.
I careen off the wall and grab the handrail for support.
Somehow, I make it to the bottom.
I stumble off the last step and spin onto the platform.

Dear God, the train is loading!
Japanese efficiency means I only have a few seconds.
I dash for the loading ramp.
The crowd parts for the charging rhino.
The automatic doors start to close.
I barrel through at full speed.
The doors slam shut on the sea bag.
My feet fly out from under me.
I crash hard on my tuckus.

A loud siren cries out as the doors retract.
The passengers glare at me in wonder.
A pretty lady helps me to my feet.
Embarrassed, I straighten my uniform.

Finding my row, I slump down in the assigned seat.
I shut my eyes and breathe.
Then concentrate on slowing my heart rate.
Relief flows over me as the train pulls away.

The stewardess takes my drink order.
Beer stat.
Digging into my pocket for payment, I only find coins.
Dread fills my heart.

It's a four hour ride.
It will require booze.

Thank Odin, Japanese coins add up fast.
A thorough accounting shows I have 5,000 yen,
About 50 bucks.
I just might make it to Hiroshima after all.

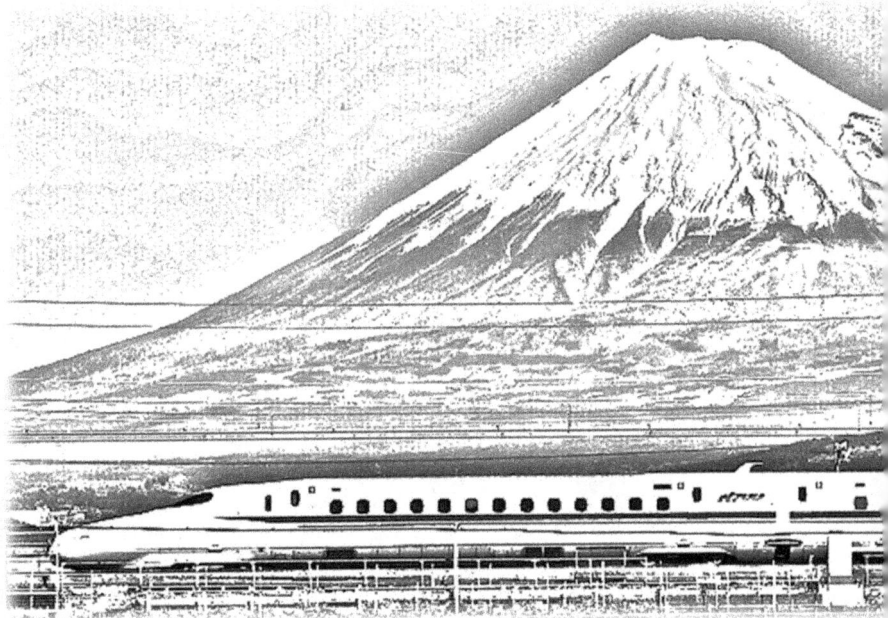

Christmas in the Brig

It was a cold, snow-covered Christmas Eve as my buddy Archie and I sat long-faced at a small bar in Iwakuni, Japan. We had been attempting to drown our sorrows with glass after glass of creamy, tasty, strong as hell, eggnog. The proprietor, an uber-happy and energetic old man, was giddy at the idea of mixing up a giant bowl of the traditional holiday spirit.

We spent the evening drinking copious amounts of sweet nog, while eating buckets of Kentucky Fried Chicken. For the life of me I never understood the Japanese's obsession with KFC. We then joined the dozen or so other native bar patrons in a round of horribly butchered Christmas carols.

The festivities served as a welcome distraction from the fact that Archie and I were spending the holidays deployed thousands of miles away from our family and friends. Christmas in Japan felt more like Valentine's Day, than a true Christian holiday. For the locals it was more of a novelty filled with couples exchanging gifts and spending an ungodly amount of money on fried chicken and mashed potatoes.

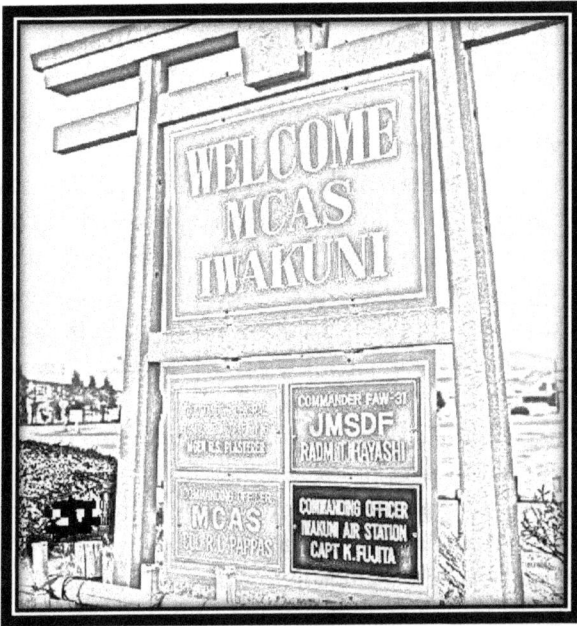

Shortly after midnight, the handful of drunkards still standing downed a final round of shots, wished each other happy holidays, and headed into the cold. The snow was falling at a slow, but steady pace, and the wind was just blustery enough to make the tips on our exposed ears turn red. The three mile hike back to the Marine Corps air station was a laborious journey.

Archie was having trouble walking a straight line, and my balance was compromised as I stumbled along with my hands buried in my pockets.

As we made the last turn toward the main entrance, we could see the flood lights shining out from the guard shack located about three blocks away. The bright lights, blinding white snow and my drunk-blurred vision began to fight against the milky liquid in my gut. My stomach lurched, and I was soon forced to pause for a moment to empty the contents of my belly.

As I looked up I noticed that Archie had veered off track and was headed perilously close to the side of the road. I yelled out his name, which startled him. His head jerked around at the sound of his name, which caused him to stumble hard to the right. He overcorrected to the left, which caused him to lose his footing and tumble down the steep incline.

I ran over to the side of the road and saw that Archie had rolled all the way down the hill and into the benjo ditch, a large open sewer system that followed the road. Luckily, the ditch was crusted with a top layer of ice that stopped Archie from falling in too deep. He had landed hard on his backside and only his butt, thighs, and hands had pushed through into the sludgy liquid. He managed to pull himself out of the filth and started crawling back up the incline. I grabbed his hand as he reached the top and heaved him over the retaining wall. As soon as he crested the top of the hill, the stench of feces and other benjo goodies hit me in a wave and I was forced unload the little remaining in my gut.

Archie had twisted his ankle in the fall, so I hooked his arm over my shoulder to assist him on the journey. Continuing on, we made it to the guard shack. Our buddy Jack was on duty, and he smiled as we approached. His smile quickly faded as the odor emanating from Archie hit his nostrils. "Holy crap man, you smell like a honey pot."

"He fell into the ditch," I offered as we hobbled past him.

Jack grabbed his nose and retreated back into the guard shack. "Be careful on your way to the barracks. Sergeant Mayfield is on duty tonight. You know he has it out for Archie."

"Thanks for the heads up, Jack."

We continued toward the barracks at a snail's pace. We only had another mile to go, but at this rate, it was going to take forever. After about 20 minutes, we reached the chow hall, which was about the halfway point. As we came up next to the large brick building we saw the dim glow of headlights headed in our direction. We decided to make a mad dash behind the chow hall to hide out. We ducked in behind one side and waited. A minute later we could see the lights slowly rounding the building.

Panic set in and we headed for the only cover available... the dumpster. We jumped into the large green dumpster landing on

black bags filled with food scraps. The smell was actually an improvement over Archie's benjo stench. Looking over the side of the dumpster, I could see Sergeant Mayfield sitting in his patrol car.

I slumped back into the dumpster.

"What's he doing?" grumbled Archie.

"He's eating something and listening to the radio. It looks like he might be a while."

Archie just shrugged and snuggled in. I pulled a fluffy bag behind my head and laid there for a while hypnotized by the large white snowflakes falling in the moonlight.

A while later, I was awoken by a loud, rather rude voice shouting my name.

"Hooch! Hooch! Wake up!"

"What man? Why are you yelling?"

"I'm yelling because your dumb ass is sleeping in a dumpster."

"Well ok. I guess that makes sense."

"For goodness sakes, you jackasses could have frozen to death out here. You're just lucky I missed the dumpster when throwing away my lunch sack."

"You really do suck at basketball," chimed in Archie as he turned onto his side and snuggled up to a large black garbage bag.

Sergeant Mayfield's face turned red. "Shut up Archie. I could take you on the court any day. Now get your drunk ass out of that dumpster. Both of you."

I slowly rolled my way to the front of the dumpster and pulled myself over the side. Mayfield put his hand on my back to prevent me from falling backwards until I could find my balance.

"I expect this from a drunk like Archie but you have always been squared away Hooch."

I just smiled. "Merry Christmas."

Mayfield rolled his eyes and turned back to the now snoring Archie. "Help me get this drunk bastard out of there before he turns into a popsicle."

After much cursing, even more grunting and a few punches to the head, Archie was dragged over the side of the dumpster.

Awake and rubbing his head Archie let out a loud belch and made a feeble attempt at standing up. He made it halfway up before slumping backward. Sergeant Mayfield and I reached out, grabbed his arms and pulled him up.

Now that he was hanging on us, his stench was palpable. "Holy crap, Archie. You smell even worse than the inside of that dumpster."

The next step was to traverse the 20 feet from the dumpster to the patrol car, which proved much harder than expected. I was barely sober enough to stand up straight and provided little help with Archie.

Sergeant Mayfield was a burly man, but it still took all his strength to drag Archie to the car. I fumbled my way to the door and managed to open it just as the duo arrived. I turned to face the pair just as Archie slumped back into my arms. Taking advantage of the momentum, Mayfield shoved hard at Archie's back causing both of us to tumble into the back seat.

The irritated MP slammed the door and jumped into the driver's seat.

"You guys are going to spend the rest of the night in the drunk tank. I'll let the captain of the guard decide what he wants to do with you in the morning."

I started to protest, but realized it was no use. Besides, Archie's room was on the third story of the barracks, and I had no desire to carry his comatose body up three flights of stairs.

The drive to the brig only lasted ten minutes, but Archie was already snoring loudly when we arrived. Sergeant Mayfield jumped out of the car and headed into the building. He returned a couple minutes later with Corporal Thompson, a good friend.

"Archie, wake up will ya'!" Shouted the sergeant as he grabbed Archie's arm and started pulling him out the door. "Come on Hooch, push!"

I pushed on Archie' back and he fell forward into the grumpy MP, knocking him backwards. Archie continued falling forward and landed in a heap on the ground. Sergeant Mayfield, Corporal Thompson, and I stood in a circle looking down at the still sleeping Archie. He looked almost peaceful laying there in a fetal position.

"Let's get him into the rack," said Mayfield. "You too, Hooch."

Five minutes later, Archie was snoring away in his metal prison bunk. The peace officers had even been kind enough to take off his boots. I tossed my boots aside, and laid back on the thin mattress. I felt relieved to be settling down for the night... Even if I was stuck in Japan, in the brig, on Christmas.

I was awakened the next morning with Archie standing over me calling my name.

"Hooch! Hooch! Wake up man... Coffee and donuts."

I sat up and took the small cup of steaming liquid and a paper plate filled with donuts.

"This prison thing isn't so bad," smiled Archie. "Warm bed, hot coffee, and fine pastries. I could get use to this."

"That's because you didn't have to listen to your snoring all night and deal with your God awful stench."

"What are you talking about? I smell like a pink unicorn."

"The ass end of a dead pink unicorn maybe," offered Corporal Thompson as he walked up to the door. "I have extra donuts and coffee if you prisoners want more."

"Thanks man, but how about the keys?" I asked.

"Sorry guys, but I can't let you out until the captain of the guard shows up. He went to Christmas Mass and will probably have lunch after. It may be a while."

"Great!" Archie slumped back onto his rack and pushed the pillow under his head. "What are we going to do for the next few hours in this tank."

Taking his cue, I pulled out a note pad I always carried with me and bummed a pen from Corporal Thompson. We spent the next two hours thinking of all the terms people used to describe prisons.

Alcatraz	Crowbar Hotel
The Asylum	Detention Center
Attica	Devils' Island
The Barricade	Dungeon
Bastille	Farm
The Big House	Gallows
Black Hole	Graybar Hotel
Brig	Guantanamo Bay
Bucket	Guardhouse
Bunkhouse	Guardroom
Cage	Hole
Can	Hoosegow
Castle	House of Correction
Cell House	House of Detention
Citadel	Ice House
Clink	Impound
Compound	Institution
Cooler	Jail
Coop	Jailhouse
Concentration Camp	Jug
Correctional Facility	The Keep

Labor Camp	Reform School
Leavenworth	The Rock
Limbo	San Quentin
Lockup	Shackle Room
The Moor	Sing Sing
Old Stoney	Slammer
The Pen	Sneezer
Penal Colony	Sponging House
Penitentiary	Stockade
Pillory	Stronghold
Pokey	The Suck
Pound	Tank
Prison	Tower
Reformatory	Wormwood

"Corporal Mayer, what the hell are you doing in here?" Bellowed a familiar voice.

I looked up to see Captain Markson staring down at me with a large smile on his face.

"I was just looking for a warm place to spend the night, sir." I responded with a hearty salute.

"Good morning, sir." Squeaked Archie, with a not-so-hearty salute.

"Holy smokes, Corporal Archibald. You look like hell. And you smell even worse."

"Merry Christmas. Happy Chanukah… Sir."

The good captain just smiled and opened the door. "Get the hell out of here. Go clean up and get to the chow hall. If you hurry there might still be some steak and lobster left for you heathens."

Archie and I looked at each other in surprise.

"You're just lucky Sergeant Mayfield forgot to log you two in last night or your names would have hit the police blotter tomorrow morning. Now get out of here."

We quickly gathered our clothes and boots and rushed out the door. God bless that irritable old sergeant and Merry Christmas to all.

Veterans Crisis Line
1-800-273-8255

The Veterans Crisis Line connects Veterans in crisis and their families and friends with qualified, caring Department of Veterans Affairs responders through a confidential toll-free hotline.

Veterans and their loved ones can call 1-800-273-8255 and *Press 1* or send a text message to 838255 to receive confidential support.

Online support and chat for veterans and their families can be found by visiting www.veteranscrisisline.net.

www.ingramcontent.com/pod-product-compliance
Lightning Source LLC
Chambersburg PA
CBHW061830040426
42447CB00012B/2907